The Greatest Bible Stories Ever Told
God's Power

Stephen Elkins
AUTHOR

Tim O'Connor
ILLUSTRATIONS

BROADMAN
& HOLMAN
PUBLISHERS
NASHVILLE, TENNESSEE

IN THE BEGINNING

Genesis 1:1 In the beginning God created the heavens and the earth.

In the beginning God created the heavens and the earth. Now the earth had no shape or form, and darkness covered the waters. And the Spirit of God was present, passing over the waters.

And God said, "Let there be light." And there was light! God saw that the light was good, and He separated the light from the dark. He called the light "day" and the darkness "night." So ended the first day of creation.

Then God said, "Let there be a visible arching sky that separates the waters." So God made the sky to separate the waters under it from the waters above it.

And everything that God spoke was accomplished in the power of His word. And so ended the second day of creation.

And God said, "Let the waters under the sky be gathered in one place and let dry land appear." And it was so. God called the dry land "earth" and the gathered waters "seas." And God saw it was good.

Then God made every kind of plant and tree, and God saw that it was good. And so ended the third day of creation.

And then with His word,
God created two great lights ... the sun to shine in the day,
and the moon to brighten the night. He also made millions
of stars. God set them in the heavens to give light to the
earth. And God saw that it was good. So ended the fourth
day of creation.

And God said, "Let the waters be filled with living creatures, and let birds fly through the skies." So God made creatures of every kind that live in the sea and every winged bird that soars above.

And God saw that it was good and He blessed them. And so ended the fifth day of God's marvelous creation.

And God said, "Let the earth produce wild animals, livestock, and all other creatures that walk or creep upon the ground."

Then God said, "Let Us make man in Our image and let them rule over all creation." So God created man in His own image; male and female He created them. God blessed them and saw that all He had made was good. And so ended the sixth day.

God had finished His work; so on the seventh day He rested.

Affirmation: I am a very special creation of God and He loves me!

DRY BONES

Ezekiel 34:26 There will be showers of blessing.

When Ezekiel the prophet arrived on the scene, the Israelite nation was held captive in Babylon. At the very same time, Jeremiah was preaching near Jerusalem. God called Ezekiel to preach a message of hope. "God has not forgotten you!" he shouted. "God does not want anyone to die with sin in their lives. Repent!"

One night, God caused Ezekiel to have a strange dream. Ezekiel was taken to the middle of a large valley. This valley was full of bones. God walked with Ezekiel back and forth through the valley. There was no end to the old dry bones.

Then the Lord asked, "Can these bones live?"
Ezekiel answered, "I don't know, Lord. Only You know!"
Then the Lord spoke again, "Ezekiel, say to these bones 'You will live. The Lord will breathe life into you and you will come to life. Then you will know that I am the Lord.'"

Ezekiel obeyed the Lord. As he was speaking, there came a noise; a rattling sound. The bones were coming back together. And as they came together, the Lord caused them to be covered with skin.

But there was no breath in them yet. Then the Lord said, "Ezekiel, tell them the Lord God says to breathe!" As soon as Ezekiel spoke the word, breath entered their bodies and they came to life. They stood up on their feet, a vast army.

Then the Lord spoke again. "Ezekiel, here's what the vision means: My people think there is no hope. They believe they are cut off from Me and dead just like those dry bones. Tell them that the Lord is going to bring them back to life and return them once again to the promised land."

Ezekiel proclaimed the message, "Dry bones can live. All things are possible with God."

Affirmation: All things are possible with God!

WORDS FROM A BURNING BUSH

Exodus 3:15 This is my name forever, the name by which I am to be remembered.

Moses grew up in an Egyptian palace, but he knew he was an Israelite by birth. One day he went out to see how his people were being treated. He saw an Egyptian beating an Israelite worker. Moses had pity on the worker and tried to stop the beating. In anger, Moses killed the slave master and hid his body in the sand.

In time, Pharaoh found out what Moses had done. He declared that Moses must die. So Moses fled to the land of Midian.

One day while Moses was leading his sheep to Horeb, also called "the mountain of God," an angel appeared from within a burning bush.

Moses thought it was very strange that this bush, though on fire, did not burn up. Then God spoke to Moses from within the burning bush. "Moses, Moses," He said. "Here I am," Moses answered. "Do not come any closer. Take off your sandals, for the place you are standing is holy ground. I am the God of Abraham, the God of Isaac, and the God of Jacob." When Moses heard this he was afraid to look at God, so he hid his face.

"I have heard the cries and prayers of My people in Egypt. So go now. I am sending you to Pharaoh to free My people and lead them out of Egypt into a good land, a land flowing with milk and honey." But Moses said to God, "Who am I that I should lead the Israelites out of Egypt?" God answered, "I will be with you."

"Who shall I tell them sent me?" Moses asked. God answered, "I AM that I AM. Tell them I AM sent you."

Moses asked, "What if they do not believe me? What if they will not listen?" Then God commanded Moses to throw down his staff. Moses obeyed and suddenly the staff became a snake. As Moses took hold of the snake, it turned back into a staff.

Then the Lord spoke to Moses again, "If they do not believe you, take some water from the Nile River and pour it on the ground. It will become blood." But Moses did not want to go and spoke again. "O Lord, I don't speak very well, and my speech is slow. Please send someone else."

This angered God and He said, "Your brother Aaron speaks very well. He will go with you. Tell him what to say and he will say it."

So Moses and his brother Aaron left for Egypt.

Affirmation:
I will go where
God sends me!

LET MY PEOPLE GO!

Moses and Aaron arrived in Egypt and went to see the Pharaoh. Moses said, "The Lord God of Israel says 'Let My people go, so that they may celebrate their deliverance and worship Me in the desert.'" Pharaoh said to Moses, "I do not believe in your God and I certainly will not obey Him. The slaves are mine and I will not let them go."

Then Pharaoh gave an order to the slave masters. "Do not give the Israelites any more straw for making bricks. Make them gather their own straw after they have finished working. But I want the number of bricks they make each day to be the same." This made their work even harder. Soon, the Israelites were beaten for falling behind in their work. Moses prayed, "O Lord, why have You brought more trouble upon Your people?" Then the Lord answered, "Because of My mighty hand, Pharaoh will let My people go. Tell My people that I am Yahweh, the Lord, and I will bring them out of bondage. They will be free and I will lead them to the land I promised Abraham."

Then the Lord said to Moses, "Go back to Pharaoh and tell him to let My people go! I will harden his heart so that he will not listen to you. But through it all, I will show Egypt that I am the true and living God. I will bring many hardships on them and soon the Israelites will be free."

Moses and Aaron returned to Pharaoh's palace and proclaimed, "The Lord has said, 'Let My people go.' Obey the Lord!" Then Aaron threw down the staff of Moses before Pharaoh and it became a snake. Pharaoh called for his magicians. When they threw down their staffs, they also became snakes. But they were amazed as Aaron's staff swallowed up theirs. But just as the Lord had said, Pharaoh would not listen.

God brought many unpleasant things upon the Egyptian people because Pharaoh would not obey God. First, Aaron dipped Moses' staff into the Nile River and it turned to blood. All of the fish died and the smell was terrible. No one could drink the water.

Seven days later Moses returned to Pharaoh and said, "The Lord says, 'Let My people go.' If you do not, I will fill the land with frogs. They will be in every house, even in your beds." Pharaoh said, "I will not free the people." So Aaron stretched out his hand with the staff, and there were frogs everywhere.

"Moses, pray that these awful frogs go away and I will let the people go," promised Pharaoh. So Moses cried out to God and the frogs went away. But Pharaoh broke his promise and did not let the people go.

"Let my people go!" cried Moses, but Pharaoh would not. So Aaron struck the ground with Moses' staff and tiny little gnats began to bite the Egyptians. Then the Lord sent swarms of flies to plague the Egyptians. They covered the entire land of Egypt, but there were no flies swarming near the Israelites.

"Moses, pray that these flies go away and I will free the people," promised Pharaoh. Moses asked the Lord to remove the flies, and God answered his prayer. But Pharaoh would not let the people go.

"Let my people go!" cried Moses, but Pharaoh would not. So the Lord sent a terrible disease that caused the horses and donkeys and camels, even the cattle and sheep to die. Then painful boils broke out on the Egyptians and their animals.

Then Moses stretched out his staff towards the sky and the Lord sent a terrible storm. There was thunder and lightning, and hailstones falling in the fields causing their crops to be beaten down. "Moses!" cried Pharaoh. "We have had enough! I will let the people go. Now pray that this terrible storm may go away." Moses knew Pharaoh would not keep his word, but to show God's power, he prayed and the stormy weather went away.

Then Moses returned to Pharaoh's palace and said, "How long will you refuse to obey the Lord? Let my people go! If you refuse, locusts will cover the ground so it cannot be seen. And they will eat every green plant left by the hailstones."

"No!" shouted Pharaoh. So Moses stretched out his staff and locusts came and covered the ground until it was black. They ate everything growing in the fields and nothing remained.

Pharaoh again called for Moses. "I have sinned, forgive me. Now pray to your God to take away these deadly locusts."

Moses prayed to the Lord and soon came a strong wind that carried the locusts into the Red Sea. Not a single locust was left anywhere in Egypt. But Pharaoh would not let the children of Israel go.

Then the Lord said, "Stretch out your staff toward the sky so that darkness will cover the land." Moses obeyed. For three days total darkness covered all of Egypt, yet the Israelites had light in their homes. Moses again said to Pharaoh, "The Lord says, 'Let My people go.'"

But Pharaoh was angry and he would not change his mind. "Get out of my sight, Moses, and don't you ever come back here again. If you do, I will kill you!" Then the Lord said to Moses, "I will send one more plague upon Egypt, then Pharaoh will let My people go."

Moses warned Pharaoh of a final plague. "The Lord has said, 'At midnight, I will go throughout Egypt and every first-born child will die. Even your son, Pharaoh, will die. And a great cry will come forth from the people.

Your rulers will bow before Me saying, *You and the Israelites must go now.'*" Then Moses left Pharaoh's palace, angry that Pharaoh refused to listen to God.

THE PASSOVER

Exodus 12:13 And when I see the blood, I will pass over you.

The Lord told Moses and Aaron how to prepare for the last plague. "Tell My people that on the tenth day of this month, each household is to select one perfect lamb. Take care of it for four days and then kill the lamb at twilight. Take some of the lamb's blood and smear it on the sides and top of your doorposts. That night, you are to eat the lamb in haste, for it is the Lord's Passover.

On that night, the Lord will pass through Egypt. But when I see the lamb's blood on your doorposts, I will pass over you. You are to remember this day forever, and celebrate your freedom."

At midnight the death angel came and all the first-born in every household in Egypt died, even Pharaoh's son. But no one died in the Israelite homes with the blood smeared over the door. Pharaoh cried to Moses, "Go! Leave as fast as you can before we all die." The Israelites were free at last.

Affirmation: It is good to obey the Lord!

THE TOWER OF BABEL

Genesis 11:9a   That is why it was called Babel - because there the LORD confused the language of the whole world.

After the great flood, Noah's children began to raise families. Their children had more children until the earth was one big family with only one language. These families began to move eastward until they came to a place called Shinar.

There the ground was just right for making bricks and there was plenty of asphalt for mortar. They said, "Let's build a grea city with a tower reaching to heaven."

So with bricks and tar the people of Shinar began building a tower to reach the very gates of heaven. When God came down and saw the tower, He was displeased. "These people believe

they can build a tower that goes to heaven without calling on My name. Come, let Us mix up their language so the people cannot speak to one another."

Immediately, their language was confused and because they could no longer understand one another, the work stopped. The Lord scattered them over all the earth. That is why to this day we call this tower the Tower of Babel, for it was there the language was confused.

Affirmation: I will worship the Lord!

27

JESUS CALMS THE STORM

Mark 4:40 He said to his disciples, "Why are you so afraid? Do you still have no faith?"

Mark tells us of another miracle Jesus did. "On another day, Jesus was teaching the people by a lake. Once again the crowds grew so big that Jesus had to get into a boat and float away from the shore. Then everyone could hear Him. There He sat and taught the people many lessons of faith."

When evening came, Jesus was very tired.
"Let's go over to the other side of the lake,"
He said. So they left the crowds
behind and set sail across the lake.
Jesus went to sleep on a cushion in
the back of the sailboat.
Suddenly, a terrible storm came up.
The waves began to break over the
sides of the boat, tossing it
back and forth.

The disciples were frightened. They thought they might die, so they turned to Jesus. "Teacher!" they shouted. "Don't You care if we drown? Help us!" Jesus got up, faced the wind and the waves and shouted, "Quiet! Be still!" And at His word, the wind stopped blowing and the waters were calm.

Then Jesus said to His disciples, "Why were you so frightened? Where is your faith?" The disciples thought, "Who is this man? Even the wind and the waves obey Him!"

Affirmation: I will run to Jesus when I am afraid!

COLLECT ALL 10

Word & Song
AUDIO BOOK

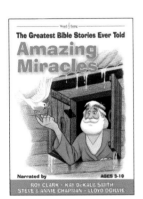
0-8054-2471-7

0-8054-2466-0

0-8054-2470-9

0-8054-2469-5

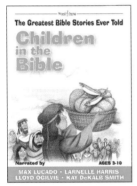
0-8054-2474-1

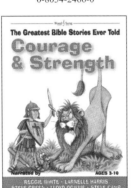
0-8054-2468-7

0-8054-2473-3

0-8054-2475-X

0-8054-2472-5

Available in Your Favorite Christian Bookstore.

0-8054-2467-9

We hope you enjoyed this Word & Song Storybook.